A Florentine Tragedy & La Sainte Courtisane by Oscar Wilde

Oscar Fingal O'Flahertie Wills Wilde was born on the 16th October 1854 in Dublin Ireland. The son of Dublin intellectuals Oscar proved himself an outstanding classicist at Dublin, then at Oxford. With his education complete Wilde moved to London and its fashionable cultural and social circles. With his biting wit, flamboyant dress, and glittering conversation, Wilde became one of the most well-known personalities of his day.

His only novel, The Picture of Dorian Gray was published in 1890 and he then moved on to writing for the stage with Salome in 1891. His society comedies produced enormous hits and turned him into one of the most successful writers of late Victorian London.

Whilst his masterpiece, The Importance of Being Earnest, was on stage in London, Wilde had the Marquess of Queensberry, the father of his lover, Lord Alfred Douglas, prosecuted for libel. The trial unearthed evidence that caused Wilde to drop his charges and led to his own arrest and trial for gross indecency. He was convicted and imprisoned for two years' hard labour. It was to break him.

On release he left for France, There he wrote his last work, The Ballad of Reading Gaol in 1898. He died destitute in Paris at the age of forty-six sipping champagne a friend had brought with the line 'Alas I am dying beyond my means'.

Here we publish two short but important examples of his plays.

Index Of Content

Preface
A Florentine Tragedy
La Sainte Courtisane
Oscar Wilde – A Short Biography

Preface

'As to my personal attitude towards criticism, I confess in brief the following: "If my works are good and of any importance whatever for the further development of art, they will maintain their place in spite of all adverse criticism and in spite of all hateful suspicions attached to my artistic intentions. If my works are of no account, the most gratifying success of the moment and the most enthusiastic approval of as augurs cannot make them endure. The waste-paper press can devour them as it has devoured many others, and I will not shed a tear . . . and the world will move on just the same."' Richard Strauss.

The contents of this volume require some explanation of an historical nature. It is scarcely realised by the present generation that Wilde's works on their first appearance, with the exception of De Profundis, were met with almost general condemnation and ridicule. The plays on their first production were grudgingly praised because their obvious success could not be ignored; but on their subsequent publication in book form they were violently assailed. That nearly all of them have held the stage is still a source of irritation among certain journalists. Salome however enjoys a singular career. As everyone knows, it was prohibited by the Censor when in rehearsal by Madame Bernhardt at the Palace Theatre in 1892. On its publication in 1893 it was greeted with greater abuse than any other of Wilde's works, and was consigned to the usual irrevocable oblivion. The accuracy of the French was freely canvassed, and of course it is obvious that the French is not that of a Frenchman. The play was passed for press, however, by no less a writer than Marcel Schwob whose letter to the Paris publisher, returning the proofs and mentioning two or three slight alterations, is still in my possession. Marcel Schwob told me some years afterwards that he thought it would have spoiled the spontaneity and character of Wilde's style if he had tried to harmonise it with the diction demanded by the French Academy. It was never composed with any idea of presentation. Madame Bernhardt happened to say she wished Wilde would write a play for her; he replied in jest that he had done so. She insisted on seeing the manuscript, and decided on its immediate production, ignorant or forgetful of the English law which prohibits the introduction of Scriptural characters on the stage. With his keen sense of the theatre Wilde would never have contrived the long speech of Salome at the end in a drama intended for the stage, even in the days of long speeches. His threat to change his nationality shortly after the Censor's interference called forth a most delightful and good-natured caricature of him by Mr. Bernard Partridge in Punch.

Wilde was still in prison in 1896 when Salome was produced by Lugne Poe at the Theatre de L'OEuvre in Paris, but except for an account in the Daily Telegraph the incident was hardly mentioned in England. I gather that the performance was only a qualified success, though Lugne Poe's triumph as Herod was generally acknowledged. In 1901, within a year of the author's death, it was produced in Berlin; from that moment it has held the European stage. It has run for a longer consecutive period in Germany than any play by any Englishman, not excepting Shakespeare. Its popularity has extended to all countries where it is not prohibited. It is performed throughout Europe, Asia and America. It is played even in Yiddish. This is remarkable in view of the many dramas by French and German writers who treat of the same theme. To none of them, however, is Wilde indebted. Flaubert, Maeterlinck (some would add Ollendorff) and Scripture, are the obvious sources on which he has freely drawn for what I do not hesitate to call the most powerful and perfect of all his dramas. But on such a point a trustee and executor may be prejudiced because it is the most valuable asset in Wilde's literary estate. Aubrey Beardsley's illustrations are too well known to need more than a passing reference. In the world of art criticism they excited almost as much attention as Wilde's drama has excited in the world of intellect.

During May 1905 the play was produced in England for the first time at a private performance by the New Stage Club. No one present will have forgotten the extraordinary tension of the audience on that occasion, those who disliked the play and its author being hypnotised by the extraordinary power of Mr. Robert Farquharson's Herod, one of the finest pieces of acting ever seen in this country. My friends the dramatic critics (and many of them are personal friends) fell on Salome with all the vigour of their predecessors twelve years before. Unaware of what was taking place in Germany, they spoke of the play as having been 'dragged from obscurity.' The Official Receiver in Bankruptcy and myself were, however, better informed. And much pleasure has been derived from reading those criticisms, all carefully preserved along with the list of receipts which were simultaneously pouring in from the German performances. To do the critics justice they never withdrew any of their printed opinions, which were all trotted out again when the play was produced privately for the second time in England by the Literary Theatre Society in 1906. In the Speaker of July 14th, 1906, however, some of the iterated misrepresentations of fact were corrected. No attempt was made to controvert the opinion of an ignorant critic: his veracity only was impugned. The powers of vaticination possessed by such judges of drama can be fairly tested in the career of Salome on the European stage, apart from the opera. In an introduction to the English translation published by Mr. John Lane it is pointed out that Wilde's confusion of Herod Antipas (Matt. xiv. 1) with Herod the Great (Matt. ii. 1) and Herod Agrippa I. (Acts xii. 23) is intentional, and follows a mediaeval convention. There is no attempt at historical accuracy or archaeological exactness. Those who saw the marvellous decor of Mr. Charles Ricketts at the second English production can form a complete idea of what Wilde intended in that respect; although the stage management was clumsy and amateurish. The great opera of Richard Strauss does not fall within my province; but the fag ends of its popularity on the Continent have been imported here oddly enough through the agency of the Palace Theatre, where Salome was originally to have been performed. Of a young lady's dancing, or of that of her rivals, I am not qualified to speak. I note merely that the critics who objected to the horror of one incident in the drama lost all self-control on seeing that incident repeated in dumb show and accompanied by fescennine corybantics. Except in 'name and borrowed notoriety' the music-hall sensation has no relation whatever to the drama which so profoundly moved the whole of Europe and the greatest living musician. The adjectives of contumely are easily transmuted into epithets of adulation, when a prominent ecclesiastic succumbs, like King Herod, to the fascination of a dancer.

It is not usually known in England that a young French naval officer, unaware that Dr. Strauss was composing an opera on the theme of Salome, wrote another music drama to accompany Wilde's text. The exclusive musical rights having been already secured by Dr. Strauss, Lieutenant Marriotte's work cannot be performed regularly. One presentation, however, was permitted at Lyons, the composer's native town, where I am told it made an extraordinary impression. In order to give English readers some faint idea of the world-wide effect of Wilde's drama, my friend Mr. Walter Ledger has prepared a short bibliography of certain English and Continental translations.

At the time of Wilde's trial the nearly completed MS. of La Sainte Courtisane was entrusted to Mrs. Leverson, the well-known novelist, who in 1897 went to Paris on purpose to restore it to the author. Wilde immediately left the only copy in a cab. A few days later he laughingly informed me of the loss, and added that a cab was a very proper place for it. I have explained elsewhere that he looked on his works with disdain in his last years, though he was always full of schemes for writing others. All my attempts to recover the lost work failed. The passages here reprinted are from some odd leaves of a first draft. The play is, of course, not unlike Salome, though it was written in English. It expanded Wilde's favourite theory that when you convert someone to an idea, you lose your faith in it; the same motive runs through Mr. W. H. Honorius the hermit, so far as I recollect the story, falls in love with the courtesan who has come to tempt him, and he reveals to her the secret of the love of God. She immediately becomes a Christian, and is murdered by robbers. Honorius the hermit goes back to Alexandria to pursue a life of pleasure. Two other similar plays Wilde invented in prison, Ahab and Isabel and Pharaoh; he would never write them down, though often importuned to do so. Pharaoh was intensely dramatic and perhaps more original than any of the group. None of these works must be confused with the manuscripts stolen from 16 Tite Street in 1895, namely, the enlarged version of Mr. W. H., the second draft of A Florentine Tragedy, and The Duchess of Padua (which, existing in a prompt copy, was of less importance than the others); nor with The Cardinal of Arragon, the manuscript of which I never saw. I scarcely think it ever existed, though Wilde used to recite proposed passages for it.

Some years after Wilde's death I was looking over the papers and letters rescued from Tite Street when I came across loose sheets of manuscript and typewriting, which I imagined were fragments of The Duchess of Padua; on putting them together in a coherent form I recognised that they belonged to the lost Florentine Tragedy. I assumed that the opening scene, though once extant, had disappeared. One day, however, Mr. Willard wrote that he possessed a typewritten fragment of a play which Wilde had submitted to him, and this he kindly forwarded for my inspection. It agreed in nearly every particular with what I had taken so much trouble to put together. This suggests that the opening scene had never been written, as Mr. Willard's version began where mine did. It was characteristic of the author to finish what he never began.

When the Literary Theatre Society produced Salome in 1906 they asked me for some other short drama by Wilde to present at the same time, as Salome does not take very long to play. I offered them the fragment of A Florentine Tragedy. By a fortunate coincidence the poet and dramatist, Mr. Thomas Sturge Moore, happened to be on the committee of this Society, and to him was entrusted the task of writing an opening scene to make the play complete. {1} It is not for me to criticise his work, but there is justification for saying that Wilde himself would have envied, with an artist's envy, such lines as

We will sup with the moon,
Like Persian princes that in Babylon
Sup in the hanging gardens of the King.

In a stylistic sense Mr. Sturge Moore has accomplished a feat in reconstruction, whatever opinions may be held of A Florentine Tragedy by Wilde's admirers or detractors. The achievement is particularly remarkable because Mr. Sturge Moore has nothing in common with Wilde other than what is shared by all real poets and dramatists: He is a landed proprietor on Parnassus, not a trespasser. In England we are more familiar with the poachers. Time and Death are of course necessary before there can come any adequate recognition of one of our most original and gifted singers. Among his works are The Vinedresser and other Poems (1899), Absalom, A Chronicle Play (1903), and The Centaur's Booty (1903). Mr. Sturge Moore is also an art critic of distinction, and his learned works on Durer (1905) and Correggio (1906) are more widely known (I am sorry to say) than his powerful and enthralling poems.

Once again I must express my obligations to Mr. Stuart Mason for revising and correcting the proofs of this new edition. Robert Ross

A Florentine Tragedy

CHARACTERS:
GUIDO BARDI, A Florentine prince
SIMONE, a merchant
BIANCA, his wife

The action takes place at Florence in the early sixteenth century.

The door opens, they separate guiltily, and the husband enters.

SIMONE
My good wife, you come slowly; were it not better
To run to meet your lord? Here, take my cloak.
Take this pack first. 'Tis heavy. I have sold nothing:
Save a furred robe unto the Cardinal's son,
Who hopes to wear it when his father dies,
And hopes that will be soon.

But who is this?
Why you have here some friend. Some kinsman doubtless,

Newly returned from foreign lands and fallen
Upon a house without a host to greet him?
I crave your pardon, kinsman. For a house
Lacking a host is but an empty thing
And void of honour; a cup without its wine,
A scabbard without steel to keep it straight,
A flowerless garden widowed of the sun.
Again I crave your pardon, my sweet cousin.

BIANCA
This is no kinsman and no cousin neither.

SIMONE
No kinsman, and no cousin! You amaze me.
Who is it then who with such courtly grace
Deigns to accept our hospitalities?

GUIDO
My name is Guido Bardi.

SIMONE
What! The son
Of that great Lord of Florence whose dim towers
Like shadows silvered by the wandering moon
I see from out my casement every night!
Sir Guido Bardi, you are welcome here,
Twice welcome. For I trust my honest wife,
Most honest if uncomely to the eye,
Hath not with foolish chatterings wearied you,
As is the wont of women.

GUIDO
Your gracious lady,
Whose beauty is a lamp that pales the stars
And robs Diana's quiver of her beams
Has welcomed me with such sweet courtesies
That if it be her pleasure, and your own,
I will come often to your simple house.
And when your business bids you walk abroad
I will sit here and charm her loneliness
Lest she might sorrow for you overmuch.
What say you, good Simone?

SIMONE
My noble Lord,
You bring me such high honour that my tongue
Like a slave's tongue is tied, and cannot say
The word it would. Yet not to give you thanks
Were to be too unmannerly. So, I thank you,
From my heart's core.

It is such things as these
That knit a state together, when a Prince
So nobly born and of such fair address,
Forgetting unjust Fortune's differences,
Comes to an honest burgher's honest home
As a most honest friend.

And yet, my Lord,
I fear I am too bold. Some other night
We trust that you will come here as a friend;
To-night you come to buy my merchandise.
Is it not so? Silks, velvets, what you will,
I doubt not but I have some dainty wares
Will woo your fancy. True, the hour is late,
But we poor merchants toil both night and day
To make our scanty gains. The tolls are high,
And every city levies its own toll,
And prentices are unskilful, and wives even
Lack sense and cunning, though Bianca here
Has brought me a rich customer to-night.
Is it not so, Bianca? But I waste time.
Where is my pack? Where is my pack, I say?
Open it, my good wife. Unloose the cords.
Kneel down upon the floor. You are better so.
Nay not that one, the other. Despatch, despatch!
Buyers will grow impatient oftentimes.
We dare not keep them waiting. Ay! 'tis that,
Give it to me; with care. It is most costly.
Touch it with care. And now, my noble Lord -
Nay, pardon, I have here a Lucca damask,
The very web of silver and the roses
So cunningly wrought that they lack perfume merely
To cheat the wanton sense. Touch it, my Lord.
Is it not soft as water, strong as steel?
And then the roses! Are they not finely woven?
I think the hillsides that best love the rose,
At Bellosguardo or at Fiesole,
Throw no such blossoms on the lap of spring,
Or if they do their blossoms droop and die.
Such is the fate of all the dainty things
That dance in wind and water. Nature herself
Makes war on her own loveliness and slays
Her children like Medea. Nay but, my Lord,
Look closer still. Why in this damask here
It is summer always, and no winter's tooth
Will ever blight these blossoms. For every ell
I paid a piece of gold. Red gold, and good,
The fruit of careful thrift.

GUIDO
Honest Simone,

Enough, I pray you. I am well content;
To-morrow I will send my servant to you,
Who will pay twice your price.

SIMONE
My generous Prince!
I kiss your hands. And now I do remember
Another treasure hidden in my house
Which you must see. It is a robe of state:
Woven by a Venetian: the stuff, cut-velvet:
The pattern, pomegranates: each separate seed
Wrought of a pearl: the collar all of pearls,
As thick as moths in summer streets at night,
And whiter than the moons that madmen see
Through prison bars at morning. A male ruby
Burns like a lighted coal within the clasp
The Holy Father has not such a stone,
Nor could the Indies show a brother to it.
The brooch itself is of most curious art,
Cellini never made a fairer thing
To please the great Lorenzo. You must wear it.
There is none worthier in our city here,
And it will suit you well. Upon one side
A slim and horned satyr leaps in gold
To catch some nymph of silver. Upon the other
Stands Silence with a crystal in her hand,
No bigger than the smallest ear of corn,
That wavers at the passing of a bird,
And yet so cunningly wrought that one would say,
It breathed, or held its breath.

Worthy Bianca,
Would not this noble and most costly robe
Suit young Lord Guido well?

Nay, but entreat him;
He will refuse you nothing, though the price
Be as a prince's ransom. And your profit
Shall not be less than mine.

BIANCA
Am I your prentice?
Why should I chaffer for your velvet robe?

GUIDO
Nay, fair Bianca, I will buy the robe,
And all things that the honest merchant has
I will buy also. Princes must be ransomed,
And fortunate are all high lords who fall
Into the white hands of so fair a foe.

SIMONE
I stand rebuked. But you will buy my wares?
Will you not buy them? Fifty thousand crowns
Would scarce repay me. But you, my Lord, shall have them
For forty thousand. Is that price too high?
Name your own price. I have a curious fancy
To see you in this wonder of the loom
Amidst the noble ladies of the court,
A flower among flowers.

They say, my lord,
These highborn dames do so affect your Grace
That where you go they throng like flies around you,
Each seeking for your favour.

I have heard also
Of husbands that wear horns, and wear them bravely,
A fashion most fantastical.

GUIDO
Simone,
Your reckless tongue needs curbing; and besides,
You do forget this gracious lady here
Whose delicate ears are surely not attuned
To such coarse music.

SIMONE
True: I had forgotten,
Nor will offend again. Yet, my sweet Lord,
You'll buy the robe of state. Will you not buy it?
But forty thousand crowns, 'tis but a trifle,
To one who is Giovanni Bardi's heir.

GUIDO
Settle this thing to-morrow with my steward,
Antonio Costa. He will come to you.
And you shall have a hundred thousand crowns
If that will serve your purpose.

SIMONE
A hundred thousand!
Said you a hundred thousand? Oh! be sure
That will for all time and in everything
Make me your debtor. Ay! from this time forth
My house, with everything my house contains
Is yours, and only yours.

A hundred thousand!
My brain is dazed. I shall be richer far
Than all the other merchants. I will buy
Vineyards and lands and gardens. Every loom

From Milan down to Sicily shall be mine,
And mine the pearls that the Arabian seas
Store in their silent caverns.

Generous Prince,
This night shall prove the herald of my love,
Which is so great that whatsoe'er you ask
It will not be denied you.

GUIDO
What if I asked
For white Bianca here?

SIMONE
You jest, my Lord;
She is not worthy of so great a Prince.
She is but made to keep the house and spin.
Is it not so, good wife? It is so. Look!
Your distaff waits for you. Sit down and spin.
Women should not be idle in their homes,
For idle fingers make a thoughtless heart.
Sit down, I say.

BIANCA
What shall I spin?

SIMONE
Oh! spin
Some robe which, dyed in purple, sorrow might wear
For her own comforting: or some long-fringed cloth
In which a new-born and unwelcome babe
Might wail unheeded; or a dainty sheet
Which, delicately perfumed with sweet herbs,
Might serve to wrap a dead man. Spin what you will;
I care not, I.

BIANCA
The brittle thread is broken,
The dull wheel wearies of its ceaseless round,
The duller distaff sickens of its load;
I will not spin to-night.

SIMONE
It matters not.
To-morrow you shall spin, and every day
Shall find you at your distaff. So Lucretia
Was found by Tarquin. So, perchance, Lucretia
Waited for Tarquin. Who knows? I have heard
Strange things about men's wives. And now, my lord,
What news abroad? I heard to-day at Pisa
That certain of the English merchants there

Would sell their woollens at a lower rate
Than the just laws allow, and have entreated
The Signory to hear them.

Is this well?
Should merchant be to merchant as a wolf?
And should the stranger living in our land
Seek by enforced privilege or craft
To rob us of our profits?

GUIDO
What should I do
With merchants or their profits? Shall I go
And wrangle with the Signory on your count?
And wear the gown in which you buy from fools,
Or sell to sillier bidders? Honest Simone,
Wool-selling or wool-gathering is for you.
My wits have other quarries.

BIANCA
Noble Lord,
I pray you pardon my good husband here,
His soul stands ever in the market-place,
And his heart beats but at the price of wool.
Yet he is honest in his common way.
To Simone
And you, have you no shame? A gracious Prince
Comes to our house, and you must weary him
With most misplaced assurance. Ask his pardon.

SIMONE
I ask it humbly. We will talk to-night
Of other things. I hear the Holy Father
Has sent a letter to the King of France
Bidding him cross that shield of snow, the Alps,
And make a peace in Italy, which will be
Worse than a war of brothers, and more bloody
Than civil rapine or intestine feuds.

GUIDO
Oh! we are weary of that King of France,
Who never comes, but ever talks of coming.
What are these things to me? There are other things
Closer, and of more import, good Simone

BIANCA
To Simone. I think you tire our most gracious guest.
What is the King of France to us? As much
As are your English merchants with their wool.

SIMONE

Is it so then? Is all this mighty world
Narrowed into the confines of this room
With but three souls for poor inhabitants?
Ay! there are times when the great universe,
Like cloth in some unskilful dyer's vat,
Shrivels into a handbreadth, and perchance
That time is now! Well! let that time be now.
Let this mean room be as that mighty stage
Whereon kings die, and our ignoble lives
Become the stakes God plays for.

I do not know
Why I speak thus. My ride has wearied me.
And my horse stumbled thrice, which is an omen
That bodes not good to any.

Alas! my lord,
How poor a bargain is this life of man,
And in how mean a market are we sold!
When we are born our mothers weep, but when
We die there is none weeps for us. No, not one.
Passes to back of stage.

BIANCA
How like a common chapman does he speak!
I hate him, soul and body. Cowardice
Has set her pale seal on his brow. His hands
Whiter than poplar leaves in windy springs,
Shake with some palsy; and his stammering mouth
Blurts out a foolish froth of empty words
Like water from a conduit.

GUIDO
Sweet Bianca,
He is not worthy of your thought or mine.
The man is but a very honest knave
Full of fine phrases for life's merchandise,
Selling most dear what he must hold most cheap,
A windy brawler in a world of words.
I never met so eloquent a fool.

BIANCA
Oh, would that Death might take him where he stands!

SIMONE
turning round.
Who spake of Death?
Let no one speak of Death.
What should Death do in such a merry house,
With but a wife, a husband, and a friend
To give it greeting? Let Death go to houses

Where there are vile, adulterous things, chaste wives
Who growing weary of their noble lords
Draw back the curtains of their marriage beds,
And in polluted and dishonoured sheets
Feed some unlawful lust. Ay! 'tis so
Strange, and yet so. YOU do not know the world.
YOU are too single and too honourable.
I know it well. And would it were not so,
But wisdom comes with winters. My hair grows grey,
And youth has left my body. Enough of that.
To-night is ripe for pleasure, and indeed,
I would be merry as beseems a host
Who finds a gracious and unlooked-for guest
Waiting to greet him. Takes up a lute.
But what is this, my lord?
Why, you have brought a lute to play to us.
Oh! play, sweet Prince. And, if I am too bold,
Pardon, but play.

GUIDO
I will not play to-night.
Some other night,

SIMONE
To Bianca You and I
Together, with no listeners but the stars,
Or the more jealous moon.

SIMONE
Nay, but my lord!
Nay, but I do beseech you. For I have heard
That by the simple fingering of a string,
Or delicate breath breathed along hollowed reeds,
Or blown into cold mouths of cunning bronze,
Those who are curious in this art can draw
Poor souls from prison-houses. I have heard also
How such strange magic lurks within these shells
That at their bidding casements open wide
And Innocence puts vine-leaves in her hair,
And wantons like a maenad. Let that pass.
Your lute I know is chaste. And therefore play:
Ravish my ears with some sweet melody;
My soul is in a prison-house, and needs
Music to cure its madness. Good Bianca,
Entreat our guest to play.

BIANCA
Be not afraid,
Our well-loved guest will choose his place and moment:
That moment is not now. You weary him
With your uncouth insistence.

GUIDO
Honest Simone,
Some other night. To-night I am content
With the low music of Bianca's voice,
Who, when she speaks, charms the too amorous air,
And makes the reeling earth stand still, or fix
His cycle round her beauty.

SIMONE
You flatter her.
She has her virtues as most women have,
But beauty in a gem she may not wear.
It is better so, perchance.

Well, my dear lord,
If you will not draw melodies from your lute
To charm my moody and o'er-troubled soul
You'll drink with me at least?

Motioning Guido to his own place.

Your place is laid.
Fetch me a stool, Bianca. Close the shutters.
Set the great bar across. I would not have
The curious world with its small prying eyes
To peer upon our pleasure.

Now, my lord,
Give us a toast from a full brimming cup.
Starts back.
What is this stain upon the cloth? It looks
As purple as a wound upon Christ's side.
Wine merely is it? I have heard it said
When wine is spilt blood is spilt also,
But that's a foolish tale.

My lord, I trust
My grape is to your liking? The wine of Naples
Is fiery like its mountains. Our Tuscan vineyards
Yield a more wholesome juice.

GUIDO
I like it well,
Honest Simone; and, with your good leave,
Will toast the fair Bianca when her lips
Have like red rose-leaves floated on this cup
And left its vintage sweeter. Taste, Bianca.

BIANCA drinks.

Oh, all the honey of Hyblean bees,
Matched with this draught were bitter!
Good Simone,
You do not share the feast.

SIMONE
It is strange, my lord,
I cannot eat or drink with you, to-night.
Some humour, or some fever in my blood,
At other seasons temperate, or some thought
That like an adder creeps from point to point,
That like a madman crawls from cell to cell,
Poisons my palate and makes appetite
A loathing, not a longing.
Goes aside.

GUIDO
Sweet Bianca,
This common chapman wearies me with words.
I must go hence. To-morrow I will come.
Tell me the hour.

BIANCA
Come with the youngest dawn!
Until I see you all my life is vain.

GUIDO
Ah! loose the falling midnight of your hair,
And in those stars, your eyes, let me behold
Mine image, as in mirrors. Dear Bianca,
Though it be but a shadow, keep me there,
Nor gaze at anything that does not show
Some symbol of my semblance. I am jealous
Of what your vision feasts on.

BIANCA
Oh! be sure
Your image will be with me always. Dear
Love can translate the very meanest thing
Into a sign of sweet remembrances.
But come before the lark with its shrill song
Has waked a world of dreamers. I will stand
Upon the balcony.

GUIDO
And by a ladder
Wrought out of scarlet silk and sewn with pearls
Will come to meet me. White foot after foot,
Like snow upon a rose-tree.

BIANCA

As you will.
You know that I am yours for love or Death.

GUIDO
Simone, I must go to mine own house.

SIMONE
So soon? Why should you? The great Duomo's bell
Has not yet tolled its midnight, and the watchmen
Who with their hollow horns mock the pale moon,
Lie drowsy in their towers. Stay awhile.
I fear we may not see you here again,
And that fear saddens my too simple heart.

GUIDO
Be not afraid,

SIMONE
I will stand
Most constant in my friendship, But to-night
I go to mine own home, and that at once.
To-morrow, sweet Bianca.

SIMONE
Well, well, so be it.
I would have wished for fuller converse with you,
My new friend, my honourable guest,
But that it seems may not be.

And besides
I do not doubt your father waits for you,
Wearying for voice or footstep. You, I think,
Are his one child? He has no other child.
You are the gracious pillar of his house,
The flower of a garden full of weeds.
Your father's nephews do not love him well
So run folks' tongues in Florence. I meant but that.
Men say they envy your inheritance
And look upon your vineyards with fierce eyes
As Ahab looked on Naboth's goodly field.
But that is but the chatter of a town
Where women talk too much.

Good-night, my lord.
Fetch a pine torch, Bianca. The old staircase
Is full of pitfalls, and the churlish moon
Grows, like a miser, niggard of her beams,
And hides her face behind a muslin mask
As harlots do when they go forth to snare
Some wretched soul in sin. Now, I will get
Your cloak and sword. Nay, pardon, my good Lord,

It is but meet that I should wait on you
Who have so honoured my poor burgher's house,
Drunk of my wine, and broken bread, and made
Yourself a sweet familiar. Oftentimes
My wife and I will talk of this fair night
And its great issues.

Why, what a sword is this.
Ferrara's temper, pliant as a snake,
And deadlier, I doubt not. With such steel,
One need fear nothing in the moil of life.
I never touched so delicate a blade.
I have a sword too, somewhat rusted now.
We men of peace are taught humility,
And to bear many burdens on our backs,
And not to murmur at an unjust world,
And to endure unjust indignities.
We are taught that, and like the patient Jew
Find profit in our pain.

Yet I remember
How once upon the road to Padua
A robber sought to take my pack-horse from me,
I slit his throat and left him. I can bear
Dishonour, public insult, many shames,
Shrill scorn, and open contumely, but he
Who filches from me something that is mine,
Ay! though it be the meanest trencher-plate
From which I feed mine appetite, oh! he
Perils his soul and body in the theft
And dies for his small sin. From what strange clay
We men are moulded!

GUIDO
Why do you speak like this?

SIMONE
I wonder, my Lord Guido, if my sword
Is better tempered than this steel of yours?
Shall we make trial? Or is my state too low
For you to cross your rapier against mine,
In jest, or earnest?

GUIDO
Naught would please me better
Than to stand fronting you with naked blade
In jest, or earnest. Give me mine own sword.
Fetch yours. To-night will settle the great issue
Whether the Prince's or the merchant's steel
Is better tempered. Was not that your word?
Fetch your own sword. Why do you tarry, sir?

SIMONE
My lord, of all the gracious courtesies
That you have showered on my barren house
This is the highest.

Bianca, fetch my sword.
Thrust back that stool and table. We must have
An open circle for our match at arms,
And good Bianca here shall hold the torch
Lest what is but a jest grow serious.

BIANCA
(To Guido). Oh! kill him, kill him!

SIMONE
Hold the torch, Bianca.
They begin to fight.

SIMONE
Have at you! Ah! Ha! would you?

He is wounded by GUIDO.

A scratch, no more. The torch was in mine eyes.
Do not look sad, Bianca. It is nothing.
Your husband bleeds, 'tis nothing. Take a cloth,
Bind it about mine arm. Nay, not so tight.
More softly, my good wife. And be not sad,
I pray you be not sad. No; take it off.
What matter if I bleed? Tears bandage off.

Again! again!
Simone disarms Guido
My gentle Lord, you see that I was right
My sword is better tempered, finer steel,
But let us match our daggers.

BIANCA
(To Guido). Kill him! kill him!

SIMONE
Put out the torch, Bianca.

Bianca puts out torch.

Now, my good Lord,
Now to the death of one, or both of us,
Or all three it may be. They fight.

There and there.

Ah, devil! do I hold thee in my grip?
Simone overpowers Guido and throws him down over table.

GUIDO
Fool! take your strangling fingers from my throat.
I am my father's only son; the State
Has but one heir, and that false enemy France
Waits for the ending of my father's line
To fall upon our city.

SIMONE
Hush! your father
When he is childless will be happier.
As for the State, I think our state of Florence
Needs no adulterous pilot at its helm.
Your life would soil its lilies.

GUIDO
Take off your hands
Take off your damned hands. Loose me, I say!

SIMONE
Nay, you are caught in such a cunning vice
That nothing will avail you, and your life
Narrowed into a single point of shame
Ends with that shame and ends most shamefully.

GUIDO
Oh! let me have a priest before I die!

SIMONE
What wouldst thou have a priest for? Tell thy sins
To God, whom thou shalt see this very night
And then no more forever. Tell thy sins
To Him who is most just, being pitiless,
Most pitiful being just. As for myself. . .

GUIDO
Oh! help me, sweet Bianca! help me, Bianca,
Thou knowest I am innocent of harm.

SIMONE
What, is there life yet in those lying lips?
Die like a dog with lolling tongue! Die! Die!
And the dumb river shall receive your corse
And wash it all unheeded to the sea.

GUIDO
Lord Christ receive my wretched soul to-night!

SIMONE

Amen to that. Now for the other.

He dies. Simone rises and looks at Bianca.
She comes towards him as one dazed with wonder and with outstretched arms.

BIANCA
Why did you not tell me you were so strong?

SIMONE
Why did you not tell me you were beautiful?

He kisses her on the mouth.

CURTAIN

La Sainte Courtisane

Act I

The scene represents the corner of a valley in the Thebaid. On the right hand of the stage is a cavern. In front of the cavern stands a great crucifix.

On the left [sand dunes].

The sky is blue like the inside of a cup of lapis lazuli. The hills are of red sand. Here and there on the hills there are clumps of thorns.

FIRST MAN: Who is she? She makes me afraid. She has a purple cloak and her hair is like threads of gold. I think she must be the daughter of the Emperor. I have heard the boatmen say that the Emperor has a daughter who wears a cloak of purple.

SECOND MAN: She has birds' wings upon her sandals, and her tunic is of the colour of green corn. It is like corn in spring when she stands still. It is like young corn troubled by the shadows of hawks when she moves. The pearls on her tunic are like many moons.

FIRST MAN: They are like the moons one sees in the water when the wind blows from the hills.

SECOND MAN: I think she is one of the gods. I think she comes from Nubia.

FIRST MAN: I am sure she is the daughter of the Emperor. Her nails are stained with henna. They are like the petals of a rose. She has come here to weep for Adonis.

SECOND MAN: She is one of the gods. I do not know why she has left her temple. The gods should not leave their temples. If she speaks to us let us not answer, and she will pass by.

FIRST MAN: She will not speak to us. She is the daughter of the Emperor.

MYRRHINA: Dwells he not here, the beautiful young hermit, he who will not look on the face of woman?

FIRST MAN: Of a truth it is here the hermit dwells.

MYRRHINA: Why will he not look on the face of woman?

SECOND MAN: We do not know.

MYRRHINA: Why do ye yourselves not look at me?

FIRST MAN: You are covered with bright stones, and you dazzle our eyes.

SECOND MAN: He who looks at the sun becomes blind. You are too bright to look at. It is not wise to look at things that are very bright. Many of the priests in the temples are blind, and have slaves to lead them.

MYRRHINA: Where does he dwell, the beautiful young hermit who will not look on the face of woman? Has he a house of reeds or a house of burnt clay or does he lie on the hillside? Or does he make his bed in the rushes?

FIRST MAN: He dwells in that cavern yonder.

MYRRHINA: What a curious place to dwell in!

FIRST MAN: Of old a centaur lived there. When the hermit came the centaur gave a shrill cry, wept and lamented, and galloped away.

SECOND MAN: No. It was a white unicorn who lived in the cave. When it saw the hermit coming the unicorn knelt down and worshipped him. Many people saw it worshipping him.

FIRST MAN: I have talked with people who saw it.

SECOND MAN: Some say he was a hewer of wood and worked for hire. But that may not be true.

MYRRHINA: What gods then do ye worship? Or do ye worship any gods? There are those who have no gods to worship. The philosophers who wear long beards and brown cloaks have no gods to worship. They wrangle with each other in the porticoes. The [ ] laugh at them.

FIRST MAN: We worship seven gods. We may not tell their names. It is a very dangerous thing to tell the names of the gods. No one should ever tell the name of his god. Even the priests who praise the gods all day long, and eat of their food with them, do not call them by their right names.

MYRRHINA: Where are these gods ye worship?

FIRST MAN: We hide them in the folds of our tunics. We do not show them to any one. If we showed them to any one they might leave us.

MYRRHINA: Where did ye meet with them?

FIRST MAN: They were given to us by an embalmer of the dead who had found them in a tomb. We served him for seven years.

MYRRHINA: The dead are terrible. I am afraid of Death.

FIRST MAN: Death is not a god. He is only the servant of the gods.

MYRRHINA: He is the only god I am afraid of. Ye have seen many of the gods?

FIRST MAN: We have seen many of them. One sees them chiefly at night time. They pass one by very swiftly. Once we saw some of the gods at daybreak. They were walking across a plain.

MYRRHINA: Once as I was passing through the market place I heard a sophist from Cilicia say that there is only one God. He said it before many people.

FIRST MAN: That cannot be true. We have ourselves seen many, though we are but common men and of no account. When I saw them I hid myself in a bush. They did me no harm.

MYRRHINA: Tell me more about the beautiful young hermit. Talk to me about the beautiful young hermit who will not look on the face of woman. What is the story of his days? What mode of life has he?

FIRST MAN: We do not understand you.

MYRRHINA: What does he do, the beautiful young hermit? Does he sow or reap? Does he plant a garden or catch fish in a net? Does he weave linen on a loom? Does he set his hand to the wooden plough and walk behind the oxen?

SECOND MAN: He being a very holy man does nothing. We are common men and of no account. We toll all day long in the sun. Sometimes the ground is very hard.

MYRRHINA: Do the birds of the air feed him? Do the jackals share their booty with him?

FIRST MAN: Every evening we bring him food. We do not think that the birds of the air feed him.

MYRRHINA: Why do ye feed him? What profit have ye in so doing?

SECOND MAN: He is a very holy man. One of the gods whom he has offended has made him mad. We think he has offended the moon.

MYRRHINA: Go and tell him that one who has come from Alexandria desires to speak with him.

FIRST MAN: We dare not tell him. This hour he is praying to his God. We pray thee to pardon us for not doing thy bidding.

MYRRHINA: Are ye afraid, of him?

FIRST MAN: We are afraid of him.

MYRRHINA: Why are ye afraid of him?

FIRST MAN: We do not know.

MYRRHINA: What is his name?

FIRST MAN: The voice that speaks to him at night time in the cavern calls to him by the name of Honorius. It was also by the name of Honorius that the three lepers who passed by once called to him. We think that his name is Honorius.

MYRRHINA: Why did the three lepers call to him?

FIRST MAN: That he might heal them.

MYRRHINA: Did he heal them?

SECOND MAN: No. They had committed some sin: it was for that reason they were lepers. Their hands and faces were like salt. One of them wore a mask of linen. He was a king's son.

MYRRHINA: What is the voice that speaks to him at night time in his cave?

FIRST MAN: We do not know whose voice it is. We think it is the voice of his God. For we have seen no man enter his cavern nor any come forth from it.

MYRRHINA: Honorius.

HONORIUS (from within): Who calls Honorius?

MYRRHINA: Come forth, Honorius.
My chamber is ceiled with cedar and odorous with myrrh.
The pillars of my bed are of cedar and the hangings are of purple.
My bed is strewn with purple and the steps are of silver.
The hangings are sewn with silver pomegranates
And the steps that are of silver are strewn with saffron and with myrrh.
My lovers hang garlands round the pillars of my house.
At night time they come with the flute players and the players of the harp.
They woo me with apples and on the pavement of my courtyard they write my name in wine.

From the uttermost parts of the world my lovers come to me.
The kings of the earth come to me and bring me presents.

When the Emperor of Byzantium heard of me he left his porphyry chamber and set sail in his galleys. His slaves bare no torches that none might know of his coming. When the King of Cyprus heard of me he sent me ambassadors. The two Kings of Libya who are brothers brought me gifts of amber.

I took the minion of Caesar from Caesar and made him my playfellow. He came to me at night in a litter. He was pale as a narcissus, and his body was like honey.

The son of the Praefect slew himself in my honour, and the Tetrarch of Cilicia scourged himself for my pleasure before my slaves.

The King of Hierapolis who is a priest and a robber set carpets for me to walk on.

Sometimes I sit in the circus and the gladiators fight beneath me. Once a Thracian who was my lover was caught in the net. I gave the signal for him to die and the whole theatre applauded. Sometimes I pass through the gymnasium and watch the young men wrestling or in the race. Their bodies are bright with oil and their brows are wreathed with willow sprays and with myrtle. They stamp their feet on the sand when they wrestle and when they run the sand follows them like a little cloud. He at whom I smile leaves his companions and follows me to my home. At other times I go down to the harbour and watch the merchants unloading their vessels. Those that come from Tyre have cloaks of silk and earrings of emerald. Those that come from Massilia have cloaks of fine wool and earrings of brass. When they see me coming they stand on the prows of their ships and call to me, but I do not answer them. I go to the little taverns where the sailors lie all day long drinking black wine and playing with dice and I sit down with them.

I made the Prince my slave, and his slave who was a Tyrian I made my lord for the space of a moon.

I put a figured ring on his finger and brought him to my house. I have wonderful things in my house.

The dust of the desert lies on your hair and your feet are scratched with thorns and your body is scorched by the sun. Come with me, Honorius, and I will clothe you in a tunic of silk. I will smear your body with myrrh and pour spikenard on your hair. I will clothe you in hyacinth and put honey in your mouth. Love -

HONORIUS: There is no love but the love of God.

MYRRHINA: Who is He whose love is greater than that of mortal men?

HONORIUS: It is He whom thou seest on the cross, Myrrhina. He is the Son of God and was born of a virgin. Three wise men who were kings brought Him offerings, and the shepherds who were lying on the hills were wakened by a great light.

The Sibyls knew of His coming. The groves and the oracles spake of Him. David and the prophets announced Him. There is no love like the love of God nor any love that can be compared to it.

The body is vile, Myrrhina. God will raise thee up with a new body which will not know corruption, and thou shalt dwell in the Courts of the Lord and see Him whose hair is like fine wool and whose feet are of brass.

MYRRHINA: The beauty. . .

HONORIUS: The beauty of the soul increases until it can see God. Therefore, Myrrhina, repent of thy sins. The robber who was crucified beside Him He brought into Paradise. [Exit.]

MYRRHINA: How strangely he spake to me. And with what scorn did he regard me. I wonder why he spake to me so strangely.

HONORIUS: Myrrhina, the scales have fallen from my eyes and I see now clearly what I did not see before. Take me to Alexandria and let me taste of the seven sins.

MYRRHINA: Do not mock me, Honorius, nor speak to me with such bitter words. For I have repented of my sins and I am seeking a cavern in this desert where I too may dwell so that my soul may become worthy to see God.

HONORIUS: The sun is setting, Myrrhina. Come with me to Alexandria.

MYRRHINA: I will not go to Alexandria.

HONORIUS: Farewell, Myrrhina.

MYRRHINA: Honorius, farewell. No, no, do not go.

I have cursed my beauty for what it has done, and cursed the wonder of my body for the evil that it has brought upon you.

Lord, this man brought me to Thy feet. He told me of Thy coming upon earth, and of the wonder of Thy birth, and the great wonder of Thy death also. By him, O Lord, Thou wast revealed to me.

HONORIUS: You talk as a child, Myrrhina, and without knowledge. Loosen your hands. Why didst thou come to this valley in thy beauty?

MYRRHINA: The God whom thou worshippest led me here that I might repent of my iniquities and know Him as the Lord.

HONORIUS: Why didst thou tempt me with words?

MYRRHINA: That thou shouldst see Sin in its painted mask and look on Death in its robe of Shame.

CURTAIN

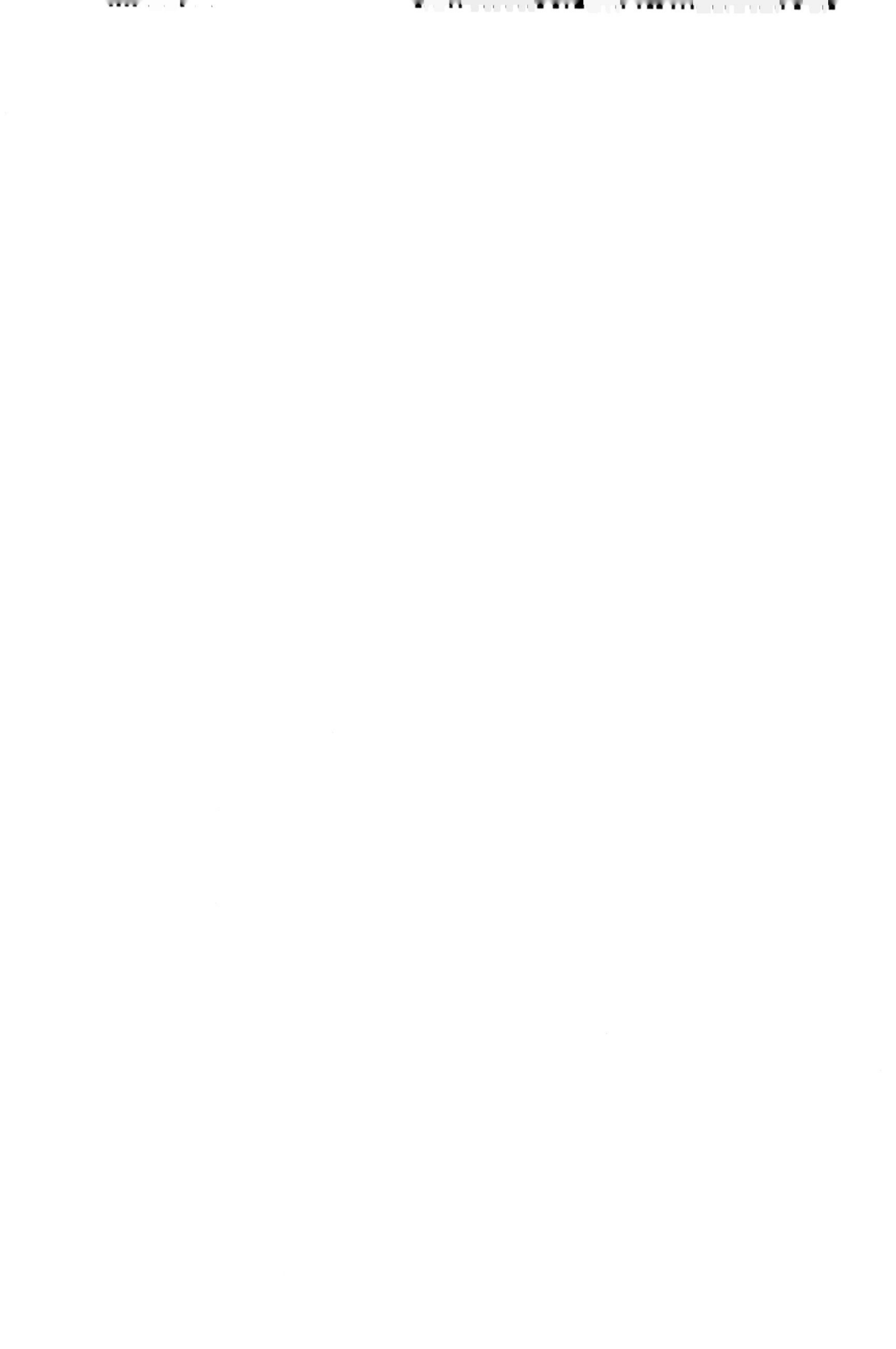

www.ingramcontent.com/pod-product-compliance
Lightning Source LLC
Chambersburg PA
CBHW070113070426
42448CB00038B/2664